UNREAL BUT REAL ANIM

UNBELIEVABLY WEIRD CREATURES

by Megan Cooley Peterson

CAPSTONE PRESS
a capstone imprint

Published by Spark, an imprint of Capstone.
1710 Roe Crest Drive, North Mankato, Minnesota 56003
capstonepub.com

Library of Congress Cataloging-in-Publication Data is available on the Library of Congress website.
ISBN 9781666355291 (hardcover)
ISBN 9781666355307 (paperback)
ISBN 9781666355314 (ebook pdf)

Summary: Full-color photos and simple, engaging text describe a variety of unusual animals, their habitats, food, and behaviors.

Image Credits
Alamy: Nature Picture Library, 15; Getty Images: Guenter Fischer, 21, Hal Beral, 25, imageBROKER/Matthias Graben, 23, Javier Fernández Sánchez, 17, NNehring, 18, Thorsten Spoerlein, 19; Shutterstock: asturfauna, 13, Don Mammoser, 7, Dr Morley Read, Cover (top), feathercollector, 27, Francesco_Ricciardi, Cover (bottom), Ian D M Robertson, 29, JeremyRichards, 5, Jiri Hrebicek, 4, meechai nongbak, 11, ZakiFF, 9

Design Elements
Shutterstock: Cassel

Editorial Credits
Editor: Erika L. Shores; Designer: Hilary Wacholz; Media Researcher: Jo Miller and Pam Mitsakos; Production Specialist: Tori Abraham

All internet sites appearing in back matter were available and accurate when this book was sent to press.

Printed in the United States   5753

TABLE OF CONTENTS

Words in **bold** are in the glossary.

WHAT KIND OF ANIMAL IS THAT?

Imagine a short giraffe with a zebra's backside. Or a seal with a giant nose that roars like a lion. Forget cute creatures. The animals in this book are just plain weird!

Being odd isn't bad. It keeps these animals safe and fed. It also helps them find a **mate**.

WEIRD IN THE SKY

BIZARRE BALLOON

The magnificent frigatebird isn't holding a red balloon. That's its neck pouch.

Males hang out in groups. They want females to notice them. They puff out their necks. The bigger, the better! Females choose the best-looking birds.

HELMETS ON

That's not a dinosaur in the tree. It's a helmeted hornbill. These birds live in **rain forests**. They have huge horns on their heads. The horn is made of the same stuff as fingernails. Males headbutt each other. They fight for the best places to nest.

FACT
Helmeted hornbills can live for 50 years in the wild.

MORE SAP, PLEASE

The lantern fly has a weird **proboscis**. It is long and red with white spots. These bugs live on fruit trees in Asia. They dip their proboscis into the trunks. Then they suck up the tree **sap**. It's all they eat.

proboscis

FLYING SCORPIONS

The scorpion fly is one weird bug. It has a long beak-like mouthpart. And its tail looks like a scorpion's. But it doesn't sting. Males use their tails to show off in front of females. They also bring females a dead bug. Without this gross gift, she might eat him.

WEIRD ON THE GROUND

OINK, OINK?

Is that a pig or a frog? The purple frog has a nose like a pig. These tiny frogs spend most of their lives underground. They come out for two weeks during the rainy season. Females lay eggs. Then it's back to life in the dirt.

FACT
The purple frog is also called the pig-nose frog.

MATA WHAT-A?

The mata mata may be the strangest turtle on Earth. These turtles have poor eyesight. Flaps of skin hang from their flat heads and long necks. These flaps help them feel for food in the water.

A mata mata has a long nose. It looks like a tube. To breathe, it sticks its nose out of the water. The turtle is almost **snorkeling**.

TONGUE BATH

What would happen if a mad scientist joined a giraffe and a zebra? You'd have an okapi. This weird African animal lives in forests. Its dark body blends in with the shadows.

FACT
Okapi are related to giraffes but not zebras.

Okapi have big ears and long, purple tongues. They lick their ears and eyes clean!

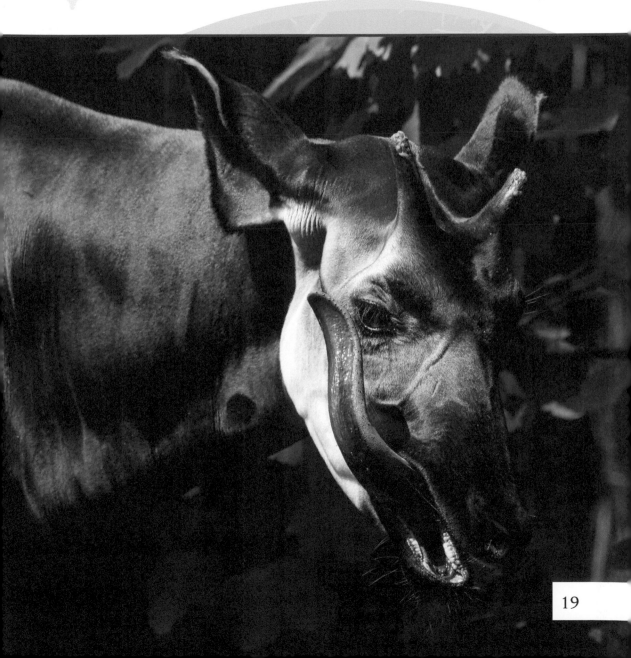

WHO ARE YOU POINTING AT?

Spiny devil katydids are the king and queen of weird. Pointy spines cover this bug's bright green body. The spines on its head look like a crown. This royally weird katydid wears these spines for a reason. Creatures get a sharp jab if they don't stay away.

WEIRD IN THE SEA

HEAR ME ROAR

Southern elephant seals spend most of their lives at sea. They come to land only once a year. And the males make a lot of noise! They fight over the best places to **breed** by roaring. Their huge noses make the sounds even louder.

> **FACT**
> Southern elephant seals are the largest of all seals.

PUCKER UP

Forget swimming. The red-lipped batfish would rather walk. It uses its fins as legs to walk along the ocean floor.

But that's not the weirdest thing about these fish. They look like they're wearing red lipstick. Their bright lips might help them find mates.

FLOATING RESTAURANT

The ocean sunfish can grow to more than 11 feet (3.4 meters) long. This giant fish is shaped like a pancake.

Many **parasites** hitch a ride on these huge fish. So how do the sunfish get rid of them? They slow down to let other fish eat the pests. Yum?

FACT
Ocean sunfish can weigh up to 5,000 pounds (2,268 kilograms). That's bigger than most cars.

LEAF ME ALONE

Can you spot the leafy sea dragon?
These fish hang out in seaweed. Flaps
of leafy skin hang from their bodies.
They blend in with their homes. Other
animals can't see these crafty creatures.

GLOSSARY

breed (BREED)—to join together to produce young

mate (MATE)—one of a pair

parasite (PAIR-uh-site)—an animal or plant that lives on other animals or plants

proboscis (pro-BAHS-kis)—a long, tube-shaped mouthpart; insects use this to drink plant juices

rain forest (RAYN FOR-ist)—a thick forest where rain falls nearly every day

sap (SAP)—a sticky, watery fluid that flows inside trees

snorkel (SNOR-kuhl)—to use a tube to breathe underwater

READ MORE

Arnold, Tedd. *Weird Animals*. New York: Scholastic Inc., 2021.

Levy, Janey. *The Beastly Elephant Seal*. New York: Gareth Stevens Publishing, 2020.

Perkins, Wendy. *Sea Dragons*. Mankato, MN: Amicus High Interest/Amicus Ink, 2018.

INTERNET SITES

The Ocean's Weirdest Creatures!
natgeokids.com/uk/discover/animals/sea-life/strange-sea-creatures/

Okapi
kids.sandiegozoowildlifealliance.org/animals/okapi

Really Weird Animals
kids.nationalgeographic.com/videos/topic/really-weird-animals

INDEX

ABOUT THE AUTHOR

Megan Cooley Peterson has been an avid reader and writer since she was a little girl. She has written nonfiction children's books about topics ranging from urban legends to gross animal facts. She lives in Minnesota with her husband and daughter.